FINGERSTYLE CURRICULUM

BEST BLUES SOLOS

Mel Bay Guitar University Series

Compiled by William Gangel
Edited by Steve Siktberg

Online Audio www.melbay.com/21365BCDEB

AUDIO CONTENTS

Audio #1

1 Blues for the Mann
2 County Line
3 Darlin'
4 Deep River Blues
5 Easy Rider Blues
6 Fare Thee Well Titanic
7 Frankie and Johnny
8 Freight Train Blues
9 A Heart Much Obliged
10 Hesitation Blues
11 Idaho Potato
12 Lemon's Jump
13 Light and Bitter
14 Microphone Fever
15 Mississippi Blues
16 Monday Morning Blues
17 Old Country Rock
18 Ragged and Dirty
19 Return to Little Rock
20 Shadyside Blues
21 Some Summer Day
22 St. James Infirmary
23 St. Louis Blues
24 Stealin'
25 Struttin' Rag
26 Sunday Street

Audio #2

1 T.N.T.
2 Tickle Dew
3 Ton of Blues
4 Tribute to Lonnie Johnson
5 Yazoo Basin Boogie

Beverly and *Blood-Red Moon* are not included on the companion audio recording.

Editor's Note

The Mel Bay Guitar University Fingerstyle Curriculum Series is designed to provide intermediate to advanced fingerstyle guitarists with a wide variety of attractive solo repertoire pieces. The material contained in these volumes is ideal for performance at professional engagements- whether concerts, cocktail parties or club dates. These solos can also be used for educational purposes and enjoyed by students and teachers alike.

Best Blues Solos provides a variety of pieces that range in style from the so called "country blues" of the old American South, to contemporary compositions written in the blues style. Guitarists will also find arrangements of well-known blues standards such as "St. Louis Blues" and "St. James Infirmary". Both standard guitar notation and tablature are provided throughout for the convenience of those who are more comfortable reading in one style or the other. Enjoy!

Table of Contents

Beverly

Indian Pacific Railroad Blues

John Fahey

Triplet feel

16
19
C
22
25
¢III
28

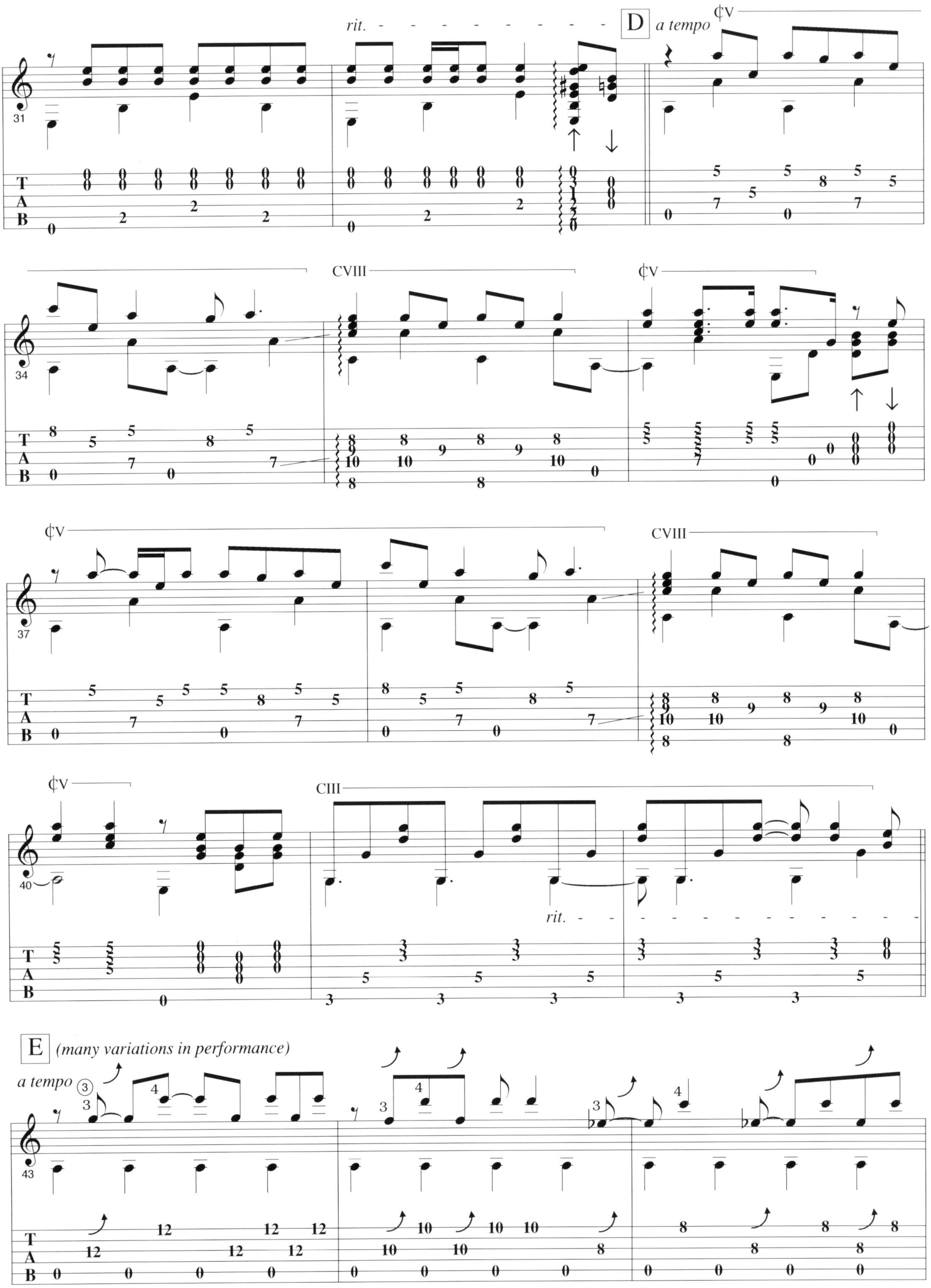
rit.
D
a tempo
¢V
CVIII
¢V
¢V
CVIII
¢V
CIII
rit.
E
(many variations in performance)
a tempo

F

"E" chord sometimes added here
rit.
G
a tempo

B2 *Variation*

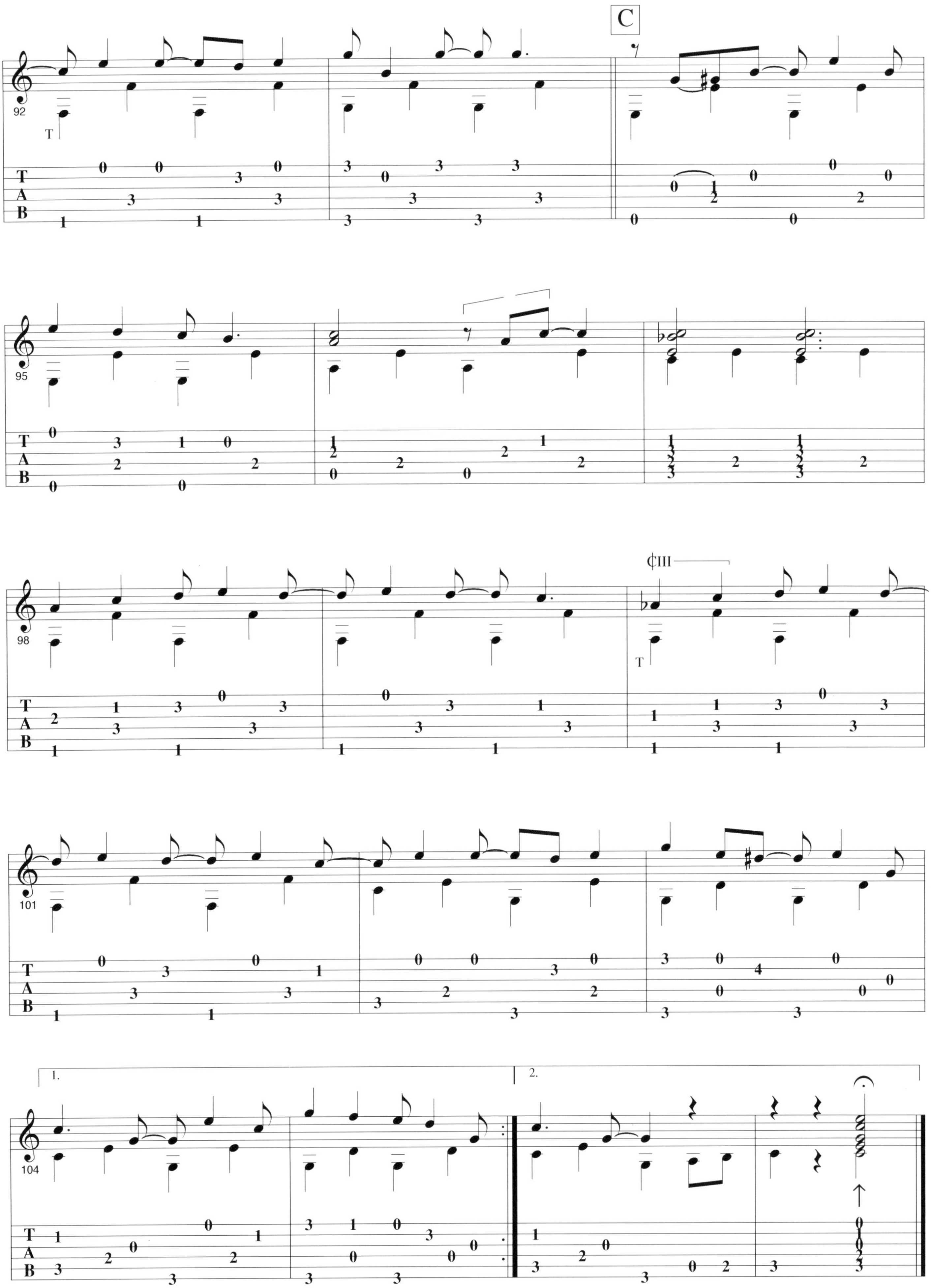
C
92
T
95
98
¢III
T
101
104
1.
2.

This page has been left blank to avoid awkward page turns

Blood-Red Moon

Dave Van Ronk

B
CV
¢III
1.
2.

CD 1
Track #1

Blues for the Mann

Stefan Grossman

¢II
A2
¢V
CV
¢V
CV

CV
To Coda
B

h.12
D. S. al Coda
Coda

CD 1
Track #2

County Line

Triplet feel

Stefan Grossman

B
To Coda
D. C. al Coda
Coda

CD 1
Track #3

Darlin'

Traditional
Arranged by Steven Eckels

Rubato, swing feel

To Coda
Swing feel, in tempo ♩ = 96
dim.
ritard.
muted bass

CIII
₵II
CVII
D. C. al Coda
ritard.

Coda
a tempo
ritard.
rubato

This page has been left blank to avoid awkward page turns

CD 1
Track #4

Deep River Blues

Traditional
Arranged by Steven Eckels

Triplet feel

p m p a p
p m p a p
₵IV
₵VII

ritard.
D.S. al Coda
Coda
ritard.
rubato
cadenza ad lib

CD 1
Track #5

Easy Rider Blues

Arranged by Stefan Grossman

CD 1
Track #6

Fare Thee Well Titanic

Capo I

Arranged by Stefan Grossman

Triplet feel

CD 1
Track #7

Frankie and Johnny

Traditional
Arranged by Steven Eckels

Triplet feel

CI
CI
CVIII

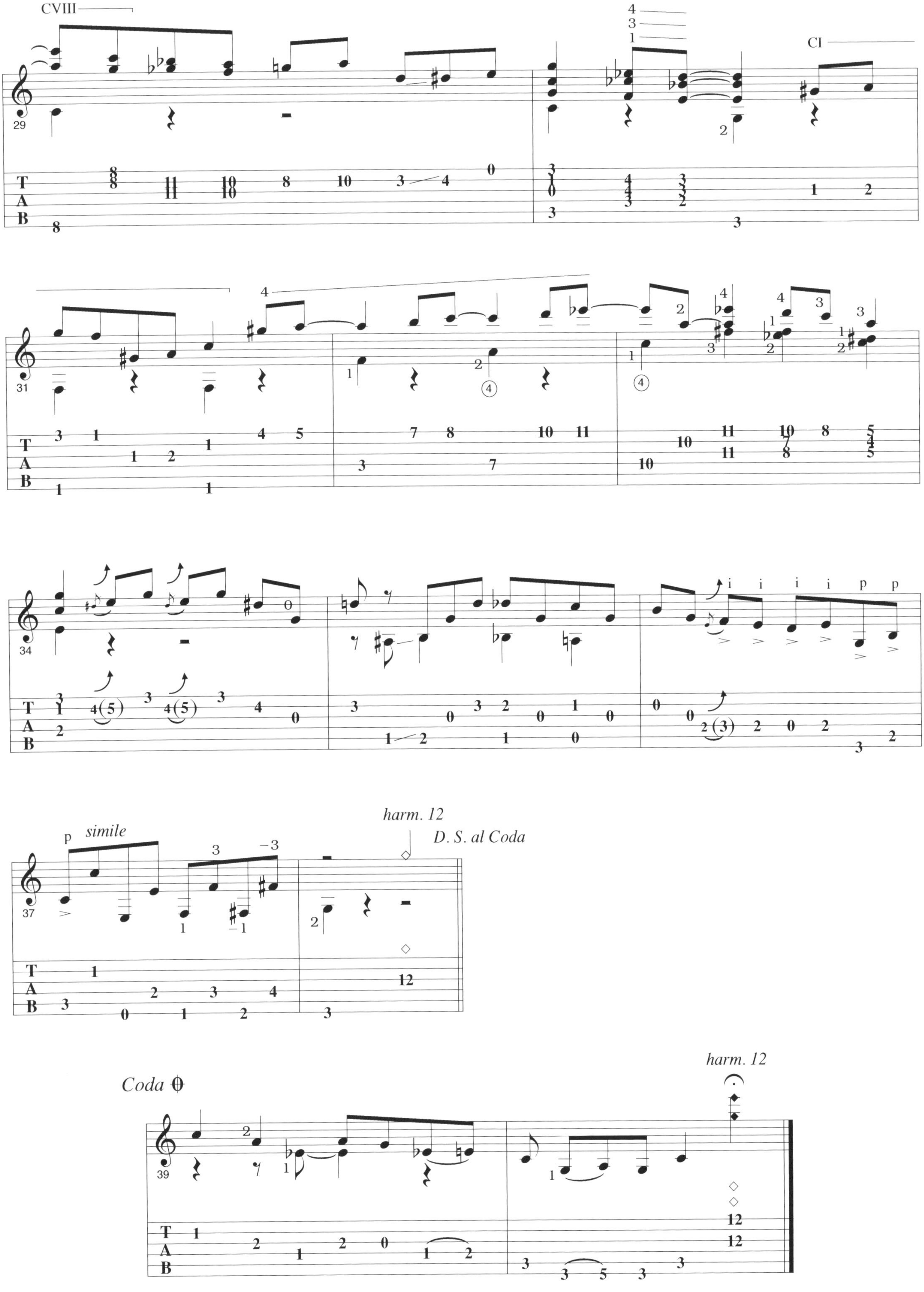
CVIII
CI
simile
harm. 12
D. S. al Coda
Coda
harm. 12

This page has been left blank to avoid awkward page turns

CD 1
Track #8

Freight Train Blues

Traditional
Arranged by Steven Eckels

Triplet feel

CII
CII
CII
CVII
T
A
B

CII
To Coda
1.
2.
CV
CII
CV
CII

1.
2.
CII
CVII
m

D. S. al Coda

Coda
ritard.
CII

CD 1
Track #9

A Heart Much Obliged

Stefan Grossman

CIV
CV
CVIII
CVIII
CIX

CVII
CII
To Coda
CV
CIV
CIII

CII
CII
CIII
CIV
₵VII
CIV
CV
D. S. al Coda
Coda
rit.
harm.

CD 1
Track #10

Hesitation Blues

Traditional
Arranged by Steven Eckels

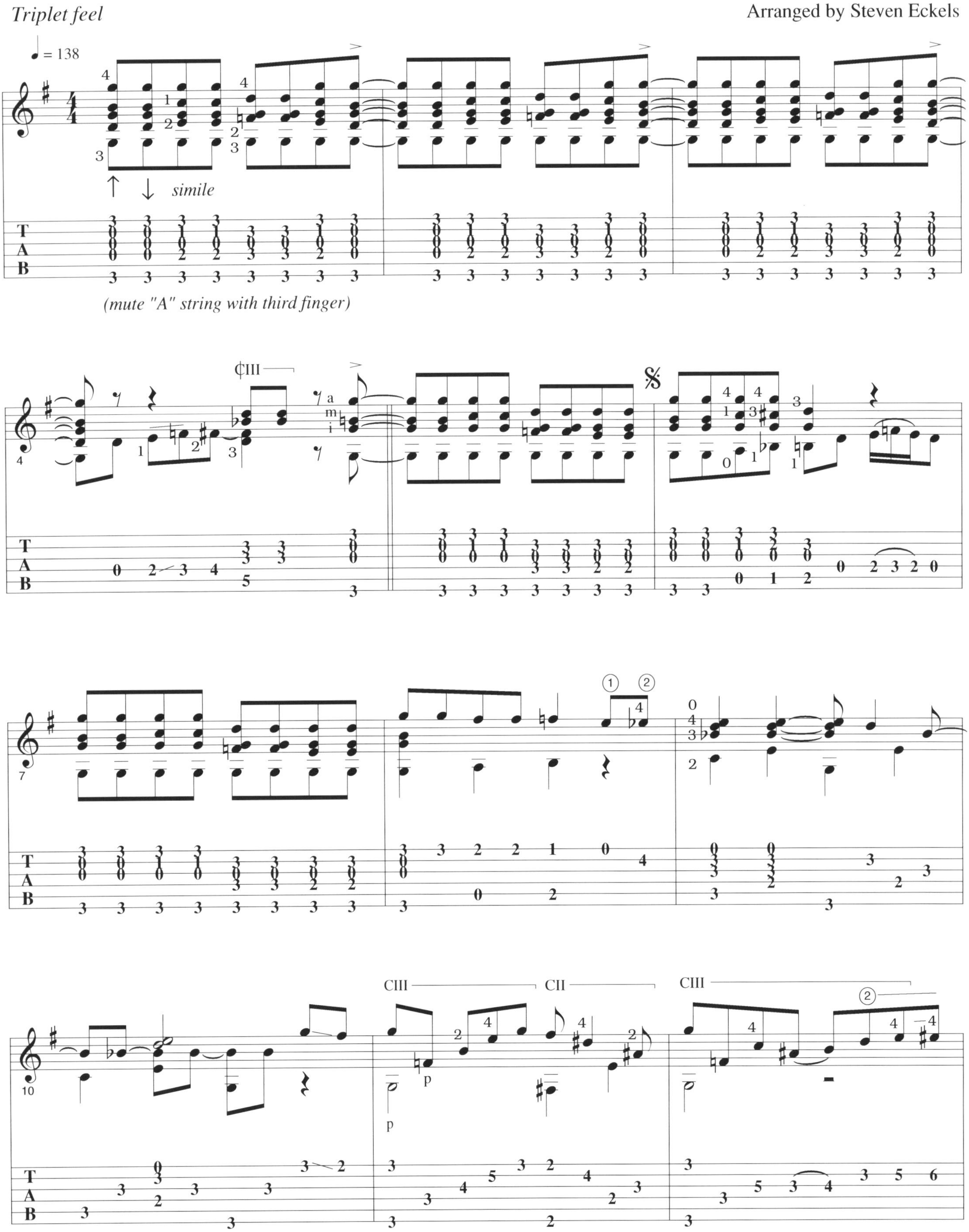

CV
CIII
To Coda
CIII

CII
¢III
¢III
CIII
T
A
B

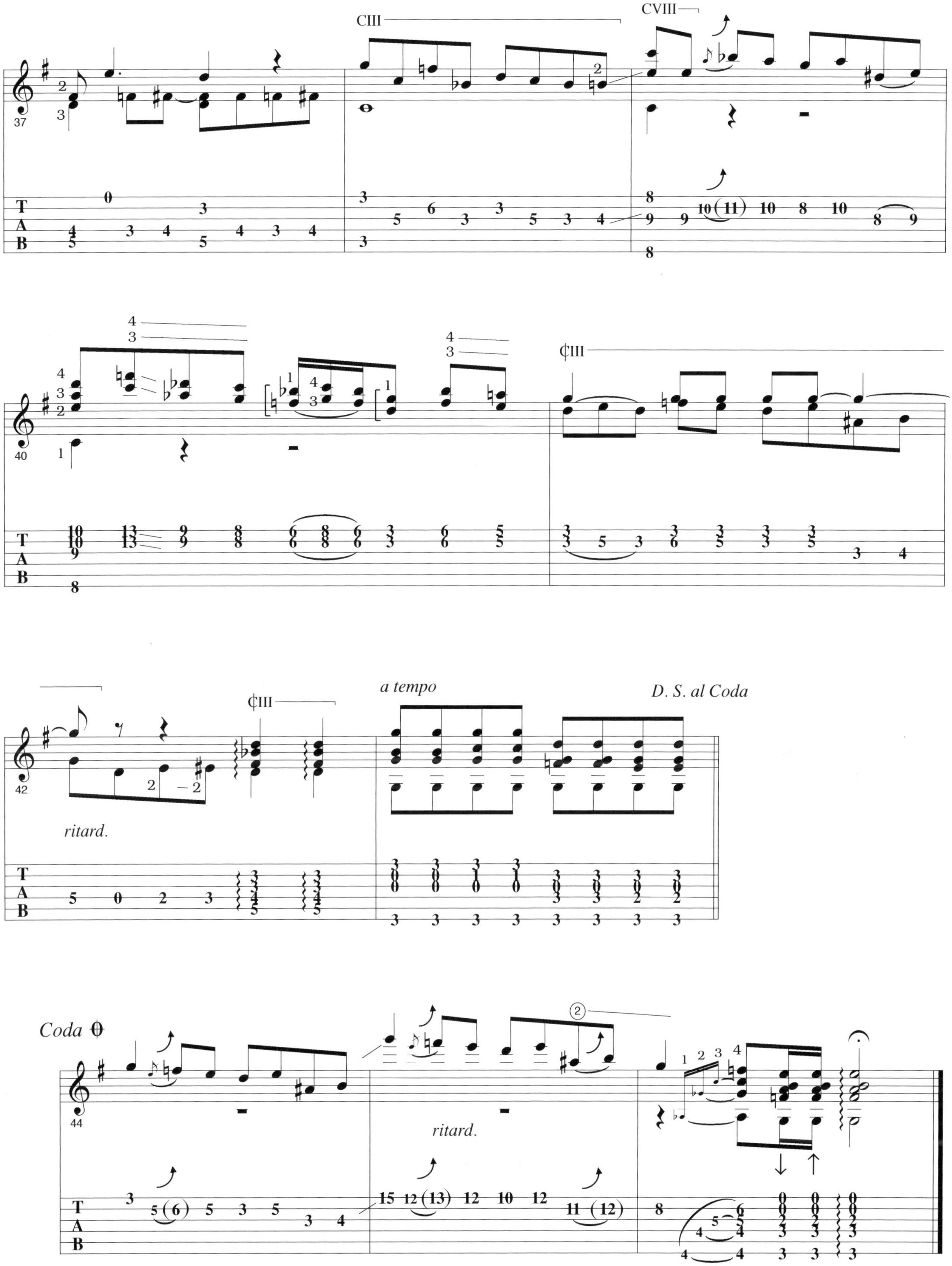
CIII
CVIII
¢III
ritard.
¢III
a tempo
D. S. al Coda
Coda
ritard.

Idaho Potato

CD 1
Track #11

Stefan Grossman

B
Verse

C
Vamp for Improvisation

D *Ending (fade after third time)*

CD 1
Track #12

Lemon's Jump

Triplet feel, ad lib

Stefan Grossman

B
CV
CV
To Coda

C
CII
CV
CV
CII
CII
D. S. al Coda
Coda

This page has been left blank to avoid awkward page turns

CD 1
Track #13

Light and Bitter

Capo I

Tom Van Bergeyk

C
molto rit.

CD 1
Track #14

Microphone Fever

Rick Ruskin

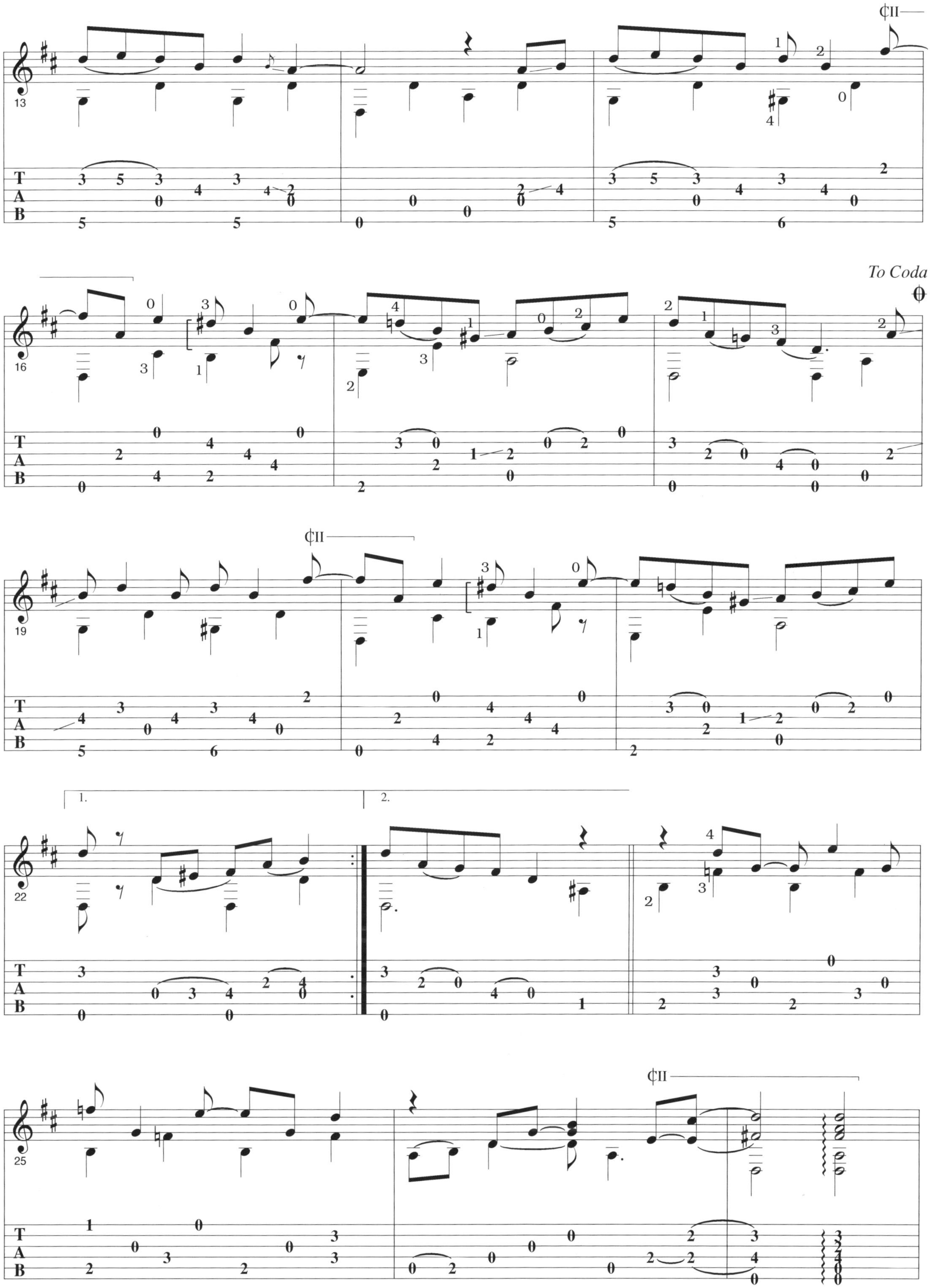
To Coda

ȼIII
D. S. al Coda

Coda
CII
40
43
46
49

CD 1
Track #15

Mississippi Blues

Arranged by Stefan Grossman

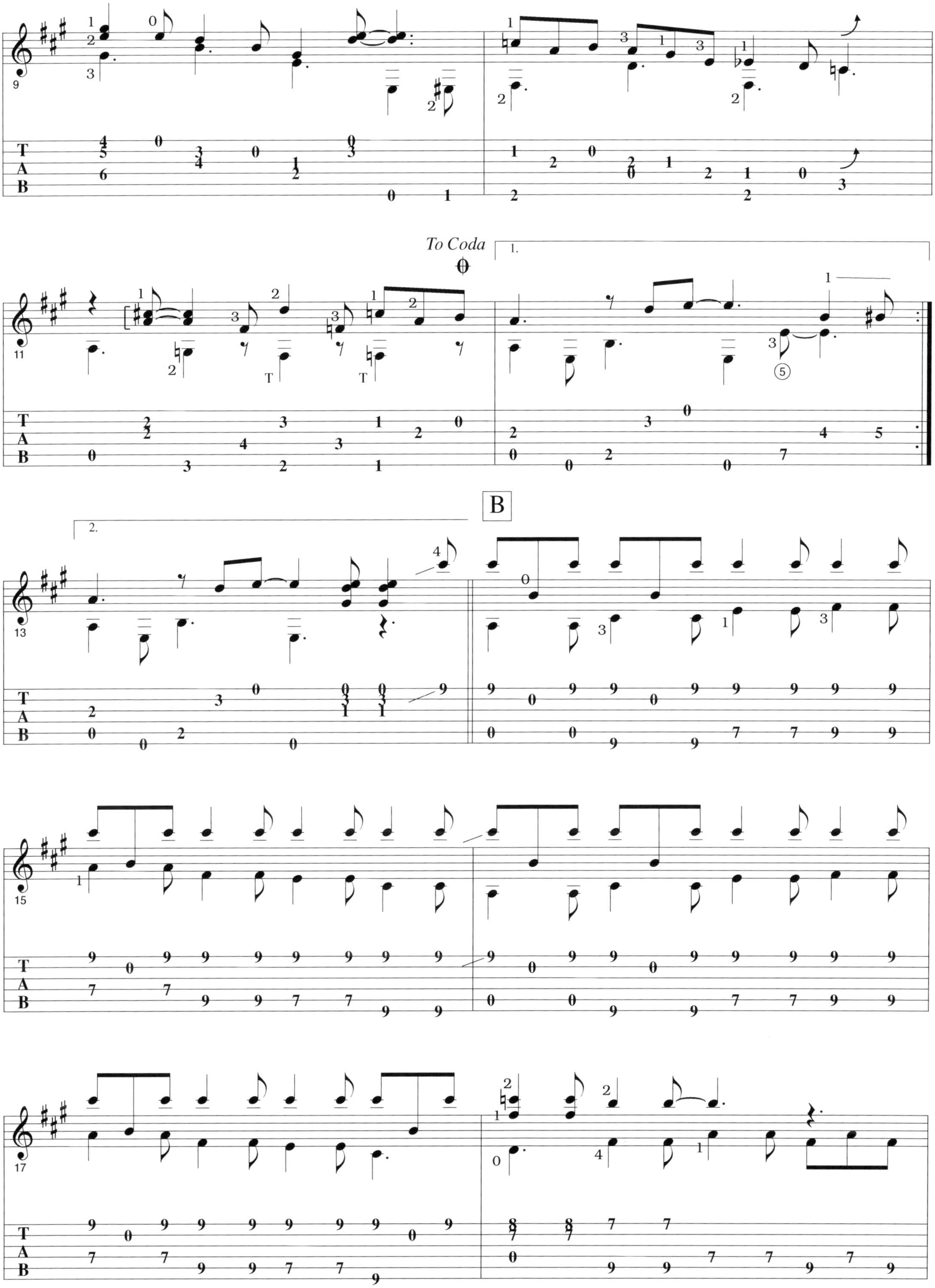
To Coda
1.
2.
B

D. S. al Coda
Coda

This page has been left blank to avoid awkward page turns

CD 1
Track #16

Monday Morning Blues

Triplet feel

by Mississippi John Hurt

12
ȻII
15
1.
ȻII
18
2.
TAB

CD 1
Track #17

Old Country Rock

Capo II

Arranged by Stefan Grossman

CII
simile
CII

CD 1
Track #18

Ragged and Dirty

Capo IV

Arranged by Stefan Grossman

Triplet feel

CD 1
Track #19

Return to Little Rock

Arranged by Stefan Grossman

D. C. al Coda
Coda

CD 1
Track #20

Shadyside Blues

Al Petteway

let ring

CII
CII

Freely

CD 1
Track #21

Some Summer Day

Capo I

John Fahey

Triplet feel

To Coda
straight eighth feel
¢VII
straight eighth feel
¢VII
straight eighth feel
¢VII
¢IX

straight eighth feel
D. C. al Coda
Coda
straight eighth feel
rit.

CD 1
Track #22

St. James Infirmary

Traditional
Arranged by Steven Eckels

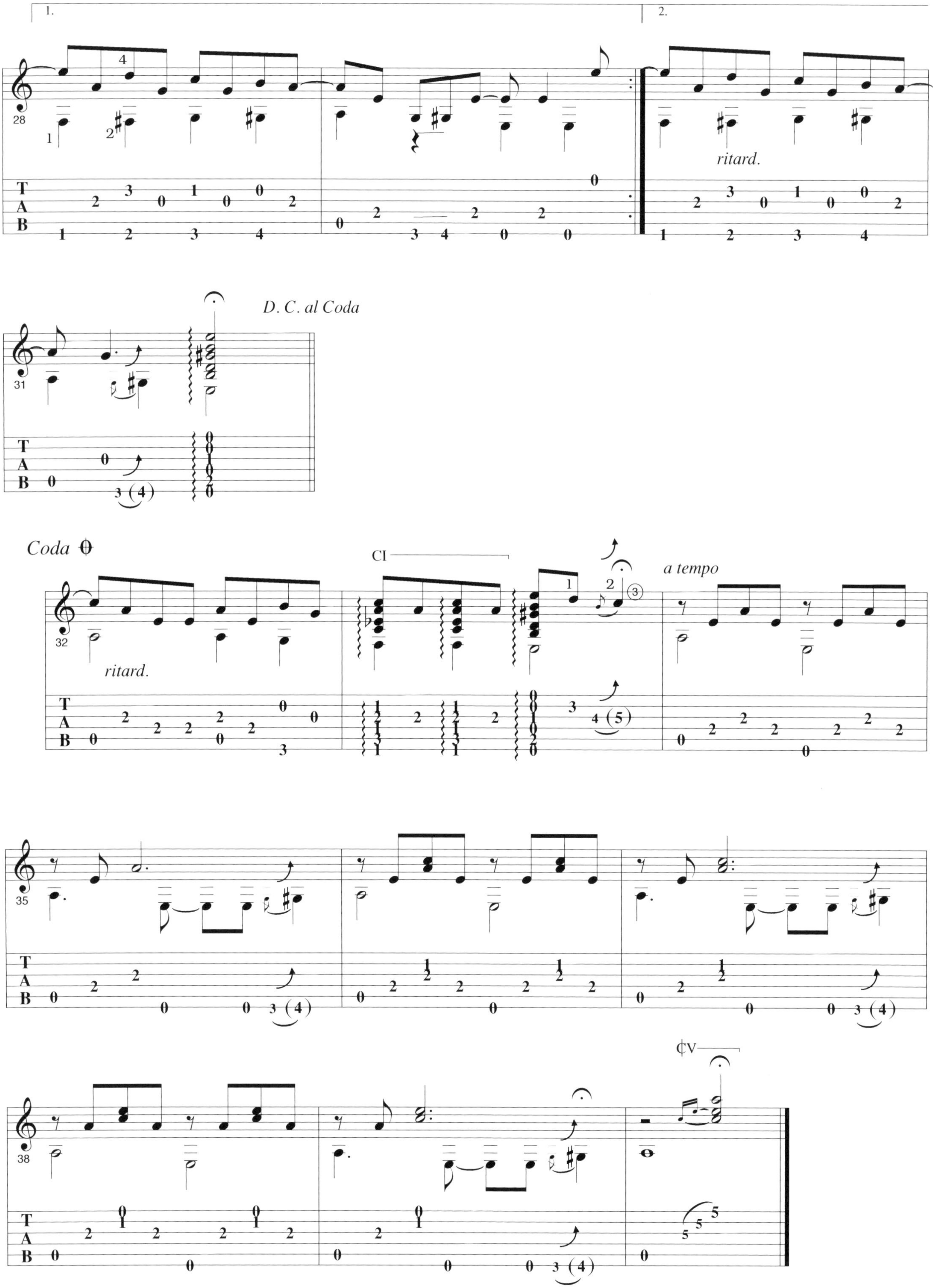

1.
2.
ritard.
D. C. al Coda
Coda
CI
a tempo
ritard.
CV

CD 1
Track #23

St. Louis Blues

W. C. Handy

(substitution for measure 4)

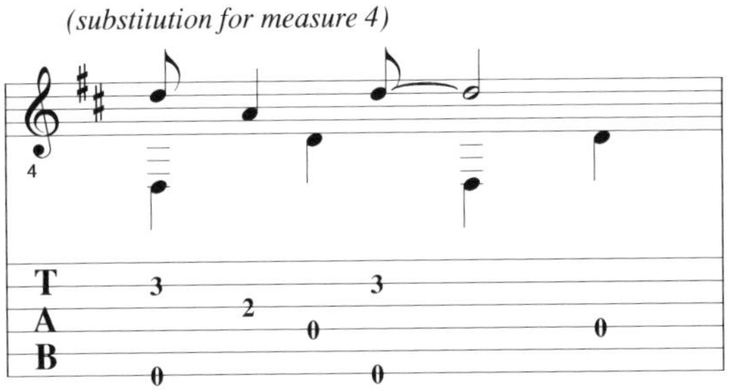

¢VII
25
28
31
34
h.7

CD 1
Track #24

Stealin'

Traditional
Arranged by Steven Eckels

Triplet feel

To Coda
CI
CIV
CVIII

CI
¢I

D. S. al Coda
ritard
Coda

CD 1
Track #25

Struttin' Rag

Capo II

by Stefan Grossman

CV
CVII
1.
2.

¢IV
¢II

Tag

Sunday Street

CD 1
Track #26

Capo III

Dave Van Ronk

18
22
A
26
30
34

C
¢VII
¢VII
A

To Coda
D
¢VII
¢VII
D. S. al Coda
Coda

CD 2
Track #1

T.N.T.

Capo I

Ton Van Bergeyk

C
Bridge

D
CX
CX
CII
D.S. al Coda
Coda
h.7
h.12

CD 2
Track #2

Tickle Dew

Capo II

by Stefan Grossman

Triplet feel

CD 2
Track #3

Ton of Blues

Capo II

by Ton Van Bergeyk

CIII
CI
B

CI
CIII
1.
2.
¢I

This page has been left blank to avoid awkward page turns

CD 2
Track #4

Tribute to Lonnie Johnson

Stefan Grossman

¢VII
¢V
1.
2.

CD 2
Track #5

Yazoo Basin Boogie

Capo V

Stefan Grossman

CII
B1
CVII
CVII
CII

To Coda
B2
CII

C

CII
D. C. al Coda
Coda
Tag